Introduction to Multipl...

There are 3 groups of bats.
There are 2 bats in each group.

$$3 \times 2 = 6$$

factors   product

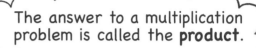

The answer to a multiplication problem is called the **product**.

Look at the picture. Write the missing factor. Then write the product.

1. $2 \times \underline{\hspace{1cm}} = \underline{\hspace{1cm}}$

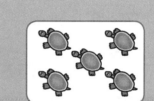

2. $2 \times \underline{\hspace{1cm}} = \underline{\hspace{1cm}}$

3. $\underline{\hspace{1cm}} \times 6 = \underline{\hspace{1cm}}$

4. $3 \times \underline{\hspace{1cm}} = \underline{\hspace{1cm}}$

5. $2 \times \underline{\hspace{1cm}} = \underline{\hspace{1cm}}$

6. $2 \times \underline{\hspace{1cm}} = \underline{\hspace{1cm}}$

Multiply by 0, 1, 2, and 3

You can also think of multiplication as **repeated addition**.

5 + 5 + 5 = __15__

3 x 5 = __15__

Write the products.

1. 2 x 1 = _____ 2 x 6 = _____
   2 x 2 = _____ 2 x 7 = _____
   2 x 3 = _____ 2 x 8 = _____
   2 x 4 = _____ 2 x 9 = _____
   2 x 5 = _____

   Count by **2s** to check
   your answers.

2. 3 x 1 = _____ 3 x 6 = _____
   3 x 2 = _____ 3 x 7 = _____
   3 x 3 = _____ 3 x 8 = _____
   3 x 4 = _____ 3 x 9 = _____
   3 x 5 = _____

   Count by **3s** to check
   your answers.

3. 1 x 1 = _____ 1 x 6 = _____
   1 x 2 = _____ 1 x 7 = _____
   1 x 3 = _____ 1 x 8 = _____
   1 x 4 = _____ 1 x 9 = _____
   1 x 5 = _____

   Hint: Any number times
   1 equals that number.

4. 0 x 1 = _____ 0 x 6 = _____
   0 x 2 = _____ 0 x 7 = _____
   0 x 3 = _____ 0 x 8 = _____
   0 x 4 = _____ 0 x 9 = _____
   0 x 5 = _____

   Hint: Any number times
   0 equals **0**.

Multiply by 4, 5, 6, and 7

Write the products.

1. 4 x 1 = _____   4 x 6 = _____
   4 x 2 = _____   4 x 7 = _____
   4 x 3 = _____   4 x 8 = _____
   4 x 4 = _____   4 x 9 = _____
   4 x 5 = _____

   Count by **4s** to check
   your answers.

2. 5 x 1 = _____   5 x 6 = _____
   5 x 2 = _____   5 x 7 = _____
   5 x 3 = _____   5 x 8 = _____
   5 x 4 = _____   5 x 9 = _____
   5 x 5 = _____

   Count by **5s** to check
   your answers.

3. 6 x 1 = _____   6 x 6 = _____
   6 x 2 = _____   6 x 7 = _____
   6 x 3 = _____   6 x 8 = _____
   6 x 4 = _____   6 x 9 = _____
   6 x 5 = _____

   Count by **6s** to check
   your answers.

4. 7 x 1 = _____   7 x 6 = _____
   7 x 2 = _____   7 x 7 = _____
   7 x 3 = _____   7 x 8 = _____
   7 x 4 = _____   7 x 9 = _____
   7 x 5 = _____

   Count by **7s** to check
   your answers.

Practice these facts.

5. 4 x 5 = _____   6. 8 x 0 = _____
7. 3 x 3 = _____   8. 5 x 4 = _____
9. 5 x 7 = _____   10. 3 x 7 = _____
11. 5 x 1 = _____   12. 4 x 8 = _____
13. 3 x 6 = _____   14. 5 x 9 = _____
15. 2 x 7 = _____   16. 2 x 5 = _____

Write the products.

1. $8 \times 1 =$ _____ $8 \times 6 =$ _____
$8 \times 2 =$ _____ $8 \times 7 =$ _____
$8 \times 3 =$ _____ $8 \times 8 =$ _____
$8 \times 4 =$ _____ $8 \times 9 =$ _____
$8 \times 5 =$ _____

Count by **8s** to check
your answers.

2. $9 \times 1 =$ _____ $9 \times 6 =$ _____
$9 \times 2 =$ _____ $9 \times 7 =$ _____
$9 \times 3 =$ _____ $9 \times 8 =$ _____
$9 \times 4 =$ _____ $9 \times 9 =$ _____
$9 \times 5 =$ _____

Count by **9s** to check
your answers.

Fill in the multiplication table. Write the products.

x	0	1	2	3	4	5	6	7	8	9
0			0							
1					4	5				
2									16	
3		3								
4			8				24			
5										45
6	0									
7		7								
8				24						
9						45				

Introduction to Division

You can use division to find the number in each group or the number of groups.

Find the number in each group:

There are 8 mice in all.
Divide the 8 mice into 2 groups.
How many are in each group? __4__

$8 \div 2 = $ __4__

Find the number of groups:

There are 8 mice in all.
There are 4 mice in each group.
How many groups of 4 are there? __2__

$8 \div 4 = $ __2__

Read the problem. Circle the correct number of groups.
Answer the question and fill in the blank(s).

1.

There are 12 in all.
There are 4 in each group.
How many groups of 4 are there? _____

$12 \div 4 = $ ____

2.

There are 15 in all.
Divide the 15 into 3 groups.
How many are in each group? _____

$15 \div 3 = $ ____

3.

There are _____ in all.
Divide the _____ into 2 groups.
How many are in each group? _____

____ $\div 2 = $ ____

4.

There are _____ in all.
Divide the _____ into 4 groups.
How many are in each group? ____

____ $\div 4 = $ ____

5.

There are _____ in all.
There are 3 in each group.
How many groups of 3 are there? _____

____ $\div 3 = $ ____

6.

There are _____ in all.
There are 6 in each group.
How many groups of 6 are there? _____

____ $\div$ ____ $= $ ____

Divide by 2 and 3

How many groups of 2 are in 16? __8__

$16 \div 2 =$ __8__

↑ dividend ↑ divisor ↑ quotient

> The answer to a division problem is called the **quotient**.

Circle groups of 2 and 3. Answer the question. Write the quotient.

1.
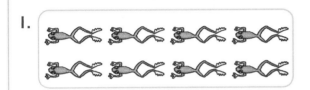

How many groups of 2 are in 8? _____

$8 \div 2 =$ _____

2.

How many groups of 2 are in 10? _____

$10 \div 2 =$ _____

3.
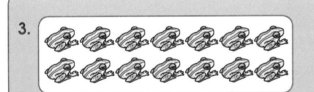

How many groups of 2 are in 14? _____

$14 \div 2 =$ _____

4.
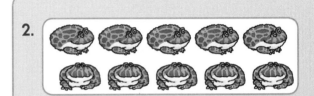

How many groups of 3 are in 15? _____

$15 \div 3 =$ _____

5.

How many groups of 3 are in 18? _____

$18 \div 3 =$ _____

6.
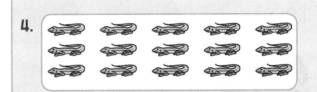

How many groups of 3 are in 21? _____

$21 \div 3 =$ _____

Divide by 4 and 5

How many groups of 5 are in 15? __3__

$15 \div 5 =$ __3__

Write the quotients.

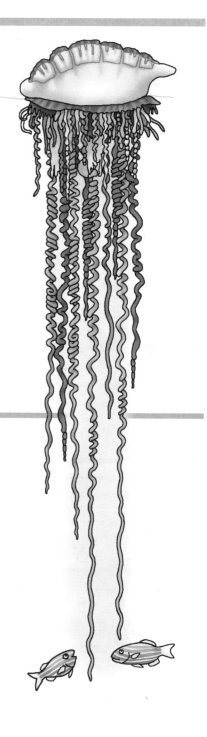

1. $4 \div 4 =$ _____
   $8 \div 4 =$ _____
   $12 \div 4 =$ _____
   $16 \div 4 =$ _____
   $20 \div 4 =$ _____
   $24 \div 4 =$ _____
   $28 \div 4 =$ _____
   $32 \div 4 =$ _____
   $36 \div 4 =$ _____

2. $5 \div 5 =$ _____
   $10 \div 5 =$ _____
   $15 \div 5 =$ _____
   $20 \div 5 =$ _____
   $25 \div 5 =$ _____
   $30 \div 5 =$ _____
   $35 \div 5 =$ _____
   $40 \div 5 =$ _____
   $45 \div 5 =$ _____

Practice these facts.

3. $6 \div 3 =$ _____
4. $4 \div 2 =$ _____
5. $10 \div 2 =$ _____
6. $15 \div 5 =$ _____
7. $20 \div 4 =$ _____
8. $14 \div 2 =$ _____
9. $20 \div 5 =$ _____
10. $12 \div 3 =$ _____
11. $25 \div 5 =$ _____
12. $18 \div 2 =$ _____
13. $8 \div 4 =$ _____
14. $10 \div 5 =$ _____
15. $16 \div 4 =$ _____
16. $12 \div 2 =$ _____
17. $21 \div 3 =$ _____
18. $28 \div 4 =$ _____

Divide by 6 and 7

Knowing multiplication facts can help you recall division facts.

Here is a multiplication fact:

$6 \times 3 = 18$

Here are two related division facts:

$18 \div 3 = 6$
$18 \div 6 = 3$

Write the quotients. Recall related multiplication facts if you need help.

1. $6 \div 6 =$ _____
   $12 \div 6 =$ _____
   $18 \div 6 =$ _____
   $24 \div 6 =$ _____
   $30 \div 6 =$ _____
   $36 \div 6 =$ _____
   $42 \div 6 =$ _____
   $48 \div 6 =$ _____
   $54 \div 6 =$ _____

2. $7 \div 7 =$ _____
   $14 \div 7 =$ _____
   $21 \div 7 =$ _____
   $28 \div 7 =$ _____
   $35 \div 7 =$ _____
   $42 \div 7 =$ _____
   $49 \div 7 =$ _____
   $56 \div 7 =$ _____
   $63 \div 7 =$ _____

Write the missing dividend, divisor, or quotient.

3. $12 \div$ _____ $= 2$

4. $56 \div$ _____ $= 8$

5. $35 \div$ _____ $= 5$

6. $54 \div 6 =$ _____

7. _____ $\div 6 = 5$

8. _____ $\div 6 = 7$

9. $49 \div 7 =$ _____

10. $7 \div$ _____ $= 1$

11. $48 \div$ _____ $= 8$

12. $36 \div$ _____ $= 6$

Divide by 8 and 9

Think of multiplication facts to find the quotients.

Write the quotients. Recall related multiplication facts if you need help.

1. $8 \div 8 =$ _____
   $16 \div 8 =$ _____
   $24 \div 8 =$ _____
   $32 \div 8 =$ _____
   $40 \div 8 =$ _____
   $48 \div 8 =$ _____
   $56 \div 8 =$ _____
   $64 \div 8 =$ _____
   $72 \div 8 =$ _____

2. $9 \div 9 =$ _____
   $18 \div 9 =$ _____
   $27 \div 9 =$ _____
   $36 \div 9 =$ _____
   $45 \div 9 =$ _____
   $54 \div 9 =$ _____
   $63 \div 9 =$ _____
   $72 \div 9 =$ _____
   $81 \div 9 =$ _____

Watch the signs!

Write the product or quotient.

3. $5 \times 8 =$ _____

4. $32 \div 8 =$ _____

5. $7 \times 9 =$ _____

6. $21 \div 7 =$ _____

7. $28 \div 4 =$ _____

8. $4 \times 7 =$ _____

9. $7 \times 6 =$ _____

10. $6 \times 6 =$ _____

11. $48 \div 6 =$ _____

12. $30 \div 6 =$ _____

13. $7 \times 8 =$ _____

14. $24 \div 3 =$ _____

15. $7 \times 7 =$ _____

16. $45 \div 5 =$ _____

17. $56 \div 7 =$ _____

18. $4 \times 9 =$ _____

19. $7 \div 7 =$ _____

20. $54 \div 9 =$ _____

$4 \div 4 = 1$

4 rabbits divided into 4 groups means that there is 1 rabbit in each group.

$4 \div 1 = 4$

4 rabbits divided into 1 group means that there are 4 rabbits in that group.

Practice the facts. Match each problem to a division rule.

Here are some division rules:

1. $3 \div 3 = \underline{} 1$

2. $13 \div 1 = \underline{}$

> Any number divided by 1 equals that number.
> **5 ÷ 1 = 5**

3. $0 \div 6 = \underline{}$

4. $10 \div 10 = \underline{}$

5. $3 \div 1 = \underline{}$

6. $0 \div 15 = \underline{}$

> Any non-zero number divided by itself equals 1.
> **5 ÷ 5 = 1**

7. $8 \div 0 = \underline{}$

8. $15 \div 15 = \underline{}$

9. $7 \div 7 = \underline{}$

10. $12 \div 0 = \underline{}$

> Zero divided by any non-zero number equals 0.
> **0 ÷ 5 = 0**

11. $0 \div 6 = \underline{}$

12. $0 \div 17 = \underline{}$

13. $9 \div 1 = \underline{}$

14. $19 \div 1 = \underline{}$

> You cannot divide by zero.
> **5 ÷ 0 =** cannot do

15. $0 \div 0 = \underline{}$

16. $20 \div 20 = \underline{}$

Write Division Facts Two Ways

There are three parts to a division problem. You can write a division problem two ways:

$$12 \div 3 = 4$$

Dividend · Divisor · Quotient

$$3\overline{)12}$$

Quotient ← 4
Dividend ← 12
Divisor ← 3

Rewrite the division problem.

1. $32 \div 4 = 8$ $\overline{)}$

2. $18 \div 2 = 9$ $\overline{)}$

3. $28 \div 7 = 4$ $\overline{)}$

4. $48 \div 6 = 8$ $\overline{)}$

Complete the problem by finding the divisor or the quotient.

5. $18 \div 3 = \underline{}$

6. $\underline{}\overline{)30}$ 6

7. $\underline{}\overline{)45}$ 5

8. $54 \div \underline{} = 9$

9. $56 \div 7 = \underline{}$

10. $7\overline{)7}$

Write the quotient.

11. $28 \div 4 = \underline{}$

12. $6\overline{)48}$

13. $24 \div 3 = \underline{}$

14. $7\overline{)49}$

15. $56 \div 8 = \underline{}$

16. $9\overline{)27}$

17. $1\overline{)9}$

18. $35 \div 5 = \underline{}$

19. $4\overline{)0}$

---

   11   Write Division Facts Two Ways (3.OA.7)

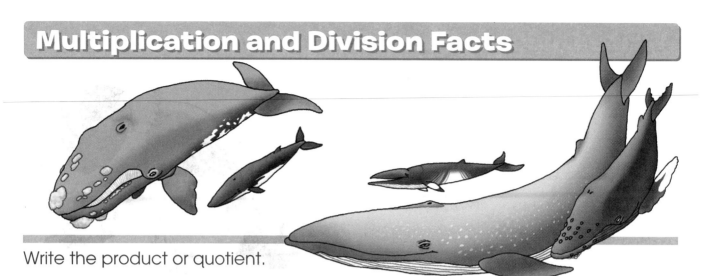

Write the product or quotient.

1. $\begin{array}{r} 8 \\ \times\ 2 \\ \hline \end{array}$

2. $\begin{array}{r} 9 \\ \times\ 0 \\ \hline \end{array}$

3. $\begin{array}{r} 5 \\ \times\ 9 \\ \hline \end{array}$

4. $\begin{array}{r} 4 \\ \times\ 8 \\ \hline \end{array}$

5. $\begin{array}{r} 5 \\ \times\ 6 \\ \hline \end{array}$

6. $2\overline{)14}$

7. $4\overline{)36}$

8. $6\overline{)42}$

9. $3\overline{)27}$

10. $5\overline{)40}$

11. $\begin{array}{r} 5 \\ \times\ 7 \\ \hline \end{array}$

12. $\begin{array}{r} 7 \\ \times\ 7 \\ \hline \end{array}$

13. $\begin{array}{r} 6 \\ \times\ 9 \\ \hline \end{array}$

14. $\begin{array}{r} 5 \\ \times\ 1 \\ \hline \end{array}$

15. $\begin{array}{r} 7 \\ \times\ 9 \\ \hline \end{array}$

16. $3\overline{)0}$

17. $6\overline{)54}$

18. $8\overline{)48}$

19. $7\overline{)56}$

20. $0\overline{)6}$

Write and solve a number sentence for the problem. Label your answer.

21. Carla wants to buy some animal stickers.
    She has 28 cents. Each sticker costs 7 cents.
    How many stickers can she buy? _____

Multiplication Clue Words

Some clue words tell you to multiply. These clue words are **how many** and **how much**. Remember that multiplying is a quicker form of addition. Use the 4 steps to help you solve the word problems.

There were 10 bikers at the start of the race. Each biker had 1 helmet. **How many** helmets were there?

$$\begin{array}{r} 10 \\ \times\ 1 \\ \hline 10 \text{ helmets} \end{array}$$

Label

There were 10 helmets.

Read and solve the problem. Label your answer.

1. There are 9 swimmers waiting for their ribbons. Each swimmer will receive 4 ribbons. How many ribbons are there altogether? _____

2. Amy swam for 5 hours every day to train for the big race. She trained for 7 days. How much time, in hours, did she spend training? _____

3. There were 8 people ready to begin the race. Each person had 3 water bottles at the finish line. How many water bottles were there at the finish line? _____

Division Clue Words

To solve division word problems, look for clue words like **share**, **how many groups**, or **how many in each group**.

Eric has **49** fish and **7** fish bowls. How many fish are in each bowl if each bowl holds the same number of fish?

$$49 \div 7 = 7$$

There are **7** fish in each fish bowl.

Read and solve the problem. Label your answer.

1. Emily has 21 birds in 7 cages. She has the same number of birds in each cage. How many birds are in each cage?

   _____

2. There are 9 elephants at the zoo. The zookeeper has 45 loaves of bread. The zookeeper will give the same number of loaves to each elephant. How many loaves will each elephant get? _____

3. Six monkeys are going to share 30 bananas. How many bananas will each monkey eat? 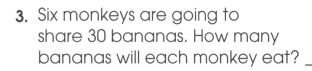 _____

4. There are 63 lions at the park. The lions are separated into 9 groups. How many lions are in each group? _____

Divide to Solve Problems (3.OA.3)   14   © School Zone Publishing Company 02031

Multiply or Divide to Solve Problems

Mrs. Smith is going on a field trip to the zoo next Tuesday at 2 o'clock. There are **20** students in the class. Each school van can carry **5** students. How many vans are needed?

Remember:
1. **Read**
2. **Decide**
3. **Solve**
4. **Check**

Read: What do you know? Which numbers do you use?

Decide: multiply or (divide)

Solve: $20 \div 5 = 4$ vans

Check: **5** students in each of **4** vans is equal to **20** students.

Read the problem. Circle multiply or divide. Solve the problem. Label your answer.

1. There are 24 pounds of fish to feed 8 seals. If each seal gets an equal amount of fish, how many pounds of fish do you give each seal?

   multiply or **divide** _____

2. Latisha has 15 animal cards. Ryan has 9 animal cards. Nicole has 3 times as many cards as Ryan. How many cards does Nicole have?

   multiply or **divide** _____

3. There are 7 chimpanzees at the zoo. A mother chimpanzee usually has a baby every 4 years. How many babies could she have in 28 years?

   multiply or **divide** _____

4. Shana has 48 flowers. On May 8th, she wants to give the same number of flowers to each of her 3 friends. How many flowers will each friend get?

   multiply or **divide** _____

Practice Multiplication Facts

Find the products to fill in the puzzle.

Across

1. $\begin{array}{r} 5 \\ \times\ 2 \\ \hline \end{array}$
2. $\begin{array}{r} 8 \\ \times\ 3 \\ \hline \end{array}$
3. $\begin{array}{r} 5 \\ \times\ 6 \\ \hline \end{array}$
4. $\begin{array}{r} 4 \\ \times\ 3 \\ \hline \end{array}$
5. $\begin{array}{r} 8 \\ \times\ 2 \\ \hline \end{array}$

6. $\begin{array}{r} 7 \\ \times\ 5 \\ \hline \end{array}$
7. $\begin{array}{r} 6 \\ \times\ 2 \\ \hline \end{array}$
8. $\begin{array}{r} 2 \\ \times\ 9 \\ \hline \end{array}$
9. $\begin{array}{r} 8 \\ \times\ 5 \\ \hline \end{array}$

10. $\begin{array}{r} 5 \\ \times\ 5 \\ \hline \end{array}$
11. $\begin{array}{r} 3 \\ \times\ 7 \\ \hline \end{array}$
12. $\begin{array}{r} 8 \\ \times\ 3 \\ \hline \end{array}$

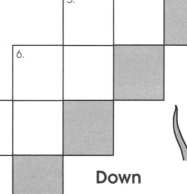

Down

1. $\begin{array}{r} 7 \\ \times\ 2 \\ \hline \end{array}$
2. $\begin{array}{r} 5 \\ \times\ 4 \\ \hline \end{array}$
3. $\begin{array}{r} 8 \\ \times\ 4 \\ \hline \end{array}$

4. $\begin{array}{r} 4 \\ \times\ 4 \\ \hline \end{array}$
5. $\begin{array}{r} 5 \\ \times\ 3 \\ \hline \end{array}$
6. $\begin{array}{r} 4 \\ \times\ 8 \\ \hline \end{array}$
7. $\begin{array}{r} 6 \\ \times\ 3 \\ \hline \end{array}$

8. $\begin{array}{r} 2 \\ \times\ 5 \\ \hline \end{array}$
9. $\begin{array}{r} 9 \\ \times\ 5 \\ \hline \end{array}$
10. $\begin{array}{r} 7 \\ \times\ 3 \\ \hline \end{array}$
11. $\begin{array}{r} 4 \\ \times\ 6 \\ \hline \end{array}$
12. $\begin{array}{r} 7 \\ \times\ 4 \\ \hline \end{array}$

Fun with Word Problems

Read each word problem.
Multiply and add to decide which numbers stand for the letters **a** and **b**.

1. Jared bought 2 bags of goldfish.
   Each bag had 3 fish in it.
   How many fish did Jared buy?

   $$\begin{array}{r} 2 \\ \times\ 3 \\ \hline \mathbf{a} \end{array}$$

   Jared had 2 more goldfish at home.
   How many goldfish did Jared have in all?

   $$\begin{array}{r} \mathbf{a} \\ +\ 2 \\ \hline \mathbf{b} \end{array}$$

   What number does the letter **a** stand for? _____

   What number does the letter **b** stand for? _____

2. Casey's mother gave her 4 books of passes to the water park.
   Each book had 8 passes in it.
   How many passes did her mother give her?

   $$\begin{array}{r} 4 \\ \times\ 8 \\ \hline \mathbf{a} \end{array}$$

   Casey's father gave her 5 more passes.
   How many passes did Casey have in all?

   $$\begin{array}{r} \mathbf{a} \\ +\ 5 \\ \hline \mathbf{b} \end{array}$$

   What number does the letter **a** stand for? _____

   What number does the letter **b** stand for? _____

3. Brody read 3 books about fish this month.
   His younger sister read 5 books this month.
   How many books in all did they read?

   $$\begin{array}{r} 3 \\ +\ 5 \\ \hline \mathbf{a} \end{array}$$

   If they read the same number of books for 3
   months, how many books in all will they read?

   $$\begin{array}{r} \mathbf{a} \\ \times\ 3 \\ \hline \mathbf{b} \end{array}$$

   What number does the letter **a** stand for? _____

   What number does the letter **b** stand for? _____

More Fun with Word Problems

Read each word problem.
Add and then divide or multiply to decide which numbers stand
for the letters **a** and **b**.

1. Dustin had 1 ripe orange at home.

   He bought 11 more oranges.

   How many oranges did Dustin have in all?

$$\begin{array}{r} 1 \\ +\ 11 \\ \hline \mathbf{a} \end{array}$$

   He wanted to divide the oranges between 4 family members.

   How many oranges did each person get?

$$\begin{array}{r} \mathbf{a} \\ \div\ 4 \\ \hline \mathbf{b} \end{array}$$

   What number does the letter **a** stand for? _____

   What number does the letter **b** stand for? _____

2. There are 15 girls in a third-grade class.

   There are 13 boys in the same class.

   How many students in all are in the class?

$$\begin{array}{r} 15 \\ +\ 13 \\ \hline \mathbf{a} \end{array}$$

   The students were divided equally into 4 groups.

   How many students were in each group?

$$\begin{array}{r} \mathbf{a} \\ \div\ 4 \\ \hline \mathbf{b} \end{array}$$

   What number does the letter **a** stand for? _____

   What number does the letter **b** stand for? _____

3. Jen earned $3.00 diving for shells yesterday.

   She earned $4.00 diving today.

   How much money did she earn in all this week?

$$\begin{array}{r} 3.00 \\ +\ 4.00 \\ \hline \mathbf{a} \end{array}$$

   If she earns that same amount for 5 weeks,

   how much money in all will she earn?

$$\begin{array}{r} \mathbf{a} \\ \times\ 5 \\ \hline \$\mathbf{b} \end{array}$$

   What number does the letter **a** stand for? _____

   What number does the letter **b** stand for? $_____

Solving Word Problems

Read each word problem. Divide, multiply, add, or subtract to decide which numbers stand for the letters **a** and **b**.

1. Three swim teams needed a bus ride.
   Each team had 10 members.

   How many members in all needed a bus ride?

$$\begin{array}{r} 3 \\ \times\ 10 \\ \hline a \end{array}$$

   Only 28 people could fit on the bus.
   How many team members could not ride the bus?

$$\begin{array}{r} a \\ -\ 28 \\ \hline b \end{array}$$

   What number does the letter **a** stand for? _____

   What number does the letter **b** stand for? _____

---

2. 12 girls arrived early to hunt for shells.
   Another 10 girls arrived late.

   How many girls in all hunted shells?

$$\begin{array}{r} 12 \\ +\ 10 \\ \hline a \end{array}$$

   The coach divided them into 2 equal numbered teams.
   How many girls were on each team?

$$\begin{array}{r} a \\ \div\ 2 \\ \hline b \end{array}$$

   What number does the letter **a** stand for? _____

   What number does the letter **b** stand for? _____

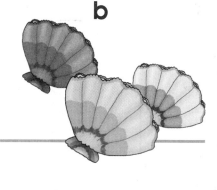

---

3. Ken invited 6 boys to his birthday party.
   He invited 4 girls to the same party.

   How many people in all did Ken invite?

$$\begin{array}{r} 6 \\ +\ 4 \\ \hline a \end{array}$$

   All but 3 came to the party.
   How many came to Ken's party?

$$\begin{array}{r} a \\ -\ 3 \\ \hline b \end{array}$$

   What number does the letter **a** stand for? _____

   What number does the letter **b** stand for? _____

Introducing Fractions

Fractions can show parts of a whole shape or a line.

Part of a Whole Shape

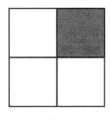

$$\frac{1}{4}$$ ← red part
← total number of parts

In a whole, each part must be the same size.

Part of a Line

$$\frac{1}{4}$$ ← number of marks from 0
← total number of marks from 0 to 1

When you work with a number line, think of the line as a ruler.

Write a fraction for the colored part or parts of the whole.

1.

_____

2.

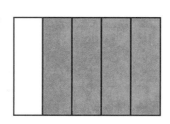

_____

3.

_____

4.

_____

5.

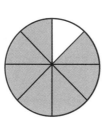

_____

6.

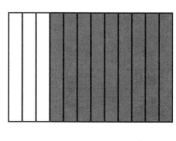

_____

Write a fraction to show where the red dot is on each number line below.

7.

_____

8.

_____

9.

_____

Equivalent Fractions

Sometimes fractions can be different numbers but name the same amount. These are called **equivalent fractions**. Look at the different ways to show fractions equivalent to $\frac{1}{4}$.

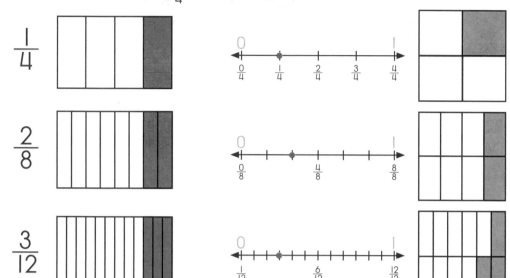

The top number of a fraction is the **numerator**. The bottom number of a fraction is the **denominator**. You can find equivalent fractions by multiplying or dividing the numerator and denominator by the same number.

$$\frac{1 \times 2 = 2}{4 \times 2 = 8} \qquad \frac{1 \times 3 = 3}{4 \times 3 = 12} \qquad \frac{3 \div 3 = 1}{12 \div 3 = 4}$$

1. Write the missing numerator.

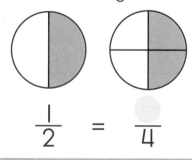

$$\frac{1}{2} = \frac{}{4}$$

2. Write the missing numerator.

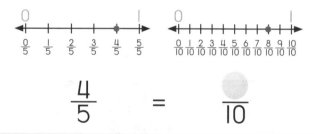

$$\frac{4}{5} = \frac{}{10}$$

Multiply or divide to find the equivalent fraction.

3. $\frac{8}{10} = \frac{4}{}$ **4.** $\frac{6}{8} = \frac{18}{}$ **5.** $\frac{8}{16} = \frac{}{4}$

Whole numbers can have equivalent fractions.

$$6 = \frac{6}{1}$$ ← 6 parts ← 1 whole

Fill in the blanks with a number.
The first one has been done for you.

1. $4 = \frac{4}{1}$

2. $7 = \frac{}{1}$

3. $9 = \frac{9}{}$

4. $34 = \frac{}{1}$

Fractions can represent whole numbers on a number line.

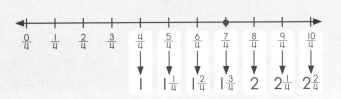

Fill in the blanks with a number.

5. $1 = \frac{}{2}$

6. $2 = \frac{}{2}$

7. $1 = \frac{}{5}$

8. $2 = \frac{}{8}$

Fractions can be compared if the numerators or denominators are the same number.

< means less than   > means more than

$\frac{1}{4}$ must be less than $\frac{3}{4}$ or $\frac{1}{4} < \frac{3}{4}$

Use the symbols =, <, or > to compare the fractions.

9. $\frac{4}{4} \bigcirc \frac{3}{3}$

10. $\frac{23}{24} \bigcirc \frac{27}{24}$

11. $\frac{5}{2} \bigcirc \frac{3}{2}$

Telling Time

Traditional clocks can have two hands. The short hand shows the hours. The long hand shows the minutes. When the long hand points to the 12, we add the word "o'clock" to the time. Digital clocks tell time more easily.

Draw hands on the clock faces to show the time.
Write the times on the digital clocks.

1. 10 o'clock

2. 34 minutes after 8 o'clock

3. 5 minutes after 6 o'clock

4. 59 minutes after 7 o'clock

Solving Word Problems with Clocks

Clocks can be used to solve word problems.
Read the word problem below.

Jonas gets out of school at **3:30** p.m. It takes him **five** minutes to get to his bike and **15** minutes to ride to his soccer practice. What time will he arrive at the soccer field?

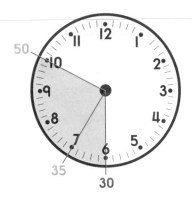

___3:50 p.m.___

Read each word problem.
Use the clock faces on the right to help you solve the problems.

1. Delia loves art. She will start her new art class next Saturday at 9:00 a.m. If it takes her 15 minutes to eat breakfast, 15 minutes to shower, and 20 minutes to ride her bike to class, what time will Delia have to wake up so she won't be late for her first class?

_____

2. Henry and his family are going to see the latest action movie this afternoon at 2:00 p.m. If it takes them 14 minutes to drive to the theater and 8 minutes to buy snacks, what time should Henry's family leave their house to get to the theater?

_____

3. If Joe takes 16 minutes to finish his math problems, 13 minutes to study his spelling words, and 25 minutes to read five chapters in a library book, what time will he finish his homework if he starts at 6:04 p.m.?

_____

Number lines can help solve word problems involving time.

If Sam practices shooting hoops with his basketball for **15** minutes, practices dribbling for **5** minutes, and runs for **10** minutes, what time will he finish if he starts at **4:45** p.m.?

_____5:15 p.m._____

Use the number lines to help you solve the word problems.

1.

Juan has chores to finish before he leaves for school. If it takes him 10 minutes to clean his room, 5 minutes to feed and give water to his dog, and 15 minutes to practice the piano, what time does Juan need to start his chores in order to leave for school at 8:45 a.m.?

_____

2.

8:45 8:50 8:55 9:00 9:05 9:10 9:15 9:20 9:25 9:30 9:35 9:40 9:45 9:50 9:55 10:00
8:45   9:00   9:15   9:30   9:45   10:00

Ann wants to play outside after she helps her little brother. If she helps him with his reading for 20 minutes, helps him wash the dog for 15 minutes, and helps him build a fort for 15 minutes, what time can she play outside if she begins helping her brother at 9:05 a.m.?

_____

3.

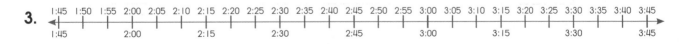

Michael's birthday party started at 2:00 p.m. If it took him 10 minutes to greet his guests, 20 minutes to open his presents, 15 minutes to eat cake and drink lemonade, and 50 minutes to play outside with his guests, what time did his guests leave?

_____

Drawing Shapes

Shapes can be grouped together according to their similarities and differences. A **quadrilateral** is any shape with four sides.

Kinds of Quadrilaterals

Rectangle	Square	Rhombus
A rectangle has all right angles. It usually has two longer sides and two shorter sides.	A square has four equal sides and all right angles.	A rhombus has four equal sides but not all right angles.

Write **rectangle, square,** or **rhombus** under each shape.

1.

   _____

2.

   _____

3.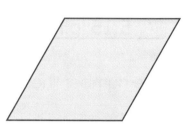

   _____

4.

   _____

5.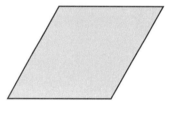

   _____

6.

   _____

7. Draw a rectangle.

8. Draw a rhombus.

9. Draw another quadrilateral.

Dividing Shapes into Halves

A shape divided in half has two equal parts.
The fraction $\frac{1}{2}$ represents each half.

one part → of the whole → $\frac{1}{2}$

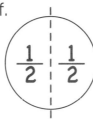

Draw a line through the middle of each shape to divide the shape in half.
Write $\frac{1}{2}$ in each section.

1.

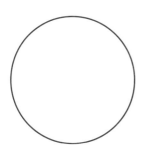

2.

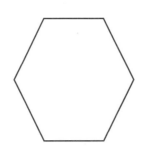

3.

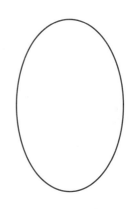

4.

5.

6.

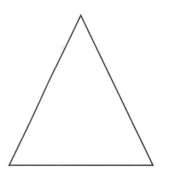

7.

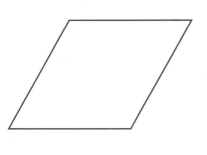

8.

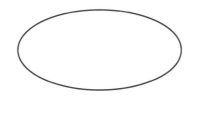

9.

Dividing Shapes into Halves (3.G.2)

Dividing Shapes into Thirds

A shape divided into thirds has three equal parts.
The fraction $\frac{1}{3}$ represents each third.

one part → $\frac{1}{3}$
of the whole →

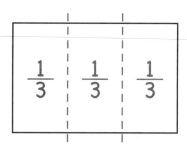

Draw lines in each shape to divide the shape into thirds.
Write $\frac{1}{3}$ in each section.

1.

2.

3.

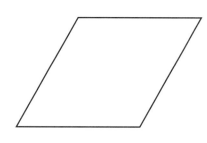

4.

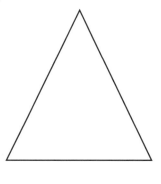

5.

6.

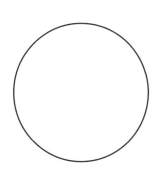

Draw these shapes and divide them into thirds.

7. Triangle

8. Rhombus

9. Rectangle

Dividing Shapes into Fourths

A shape divided into fourths has four equal parts.
The fraction $\frac{1}{4}$ represents each fourth.

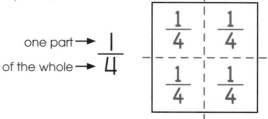

one part → $\frac{1}{4}$ ← of the whole

Draw lines in each shape to divide the shape into fourths.
Write $\frac{1}{4}$ in each section.

1.

2.

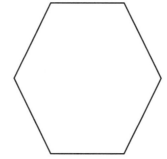

3.

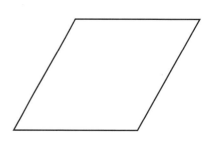

4.

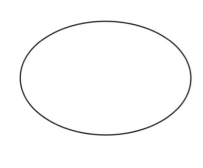

5.

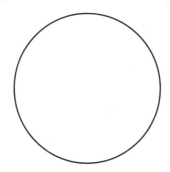

6.

7.

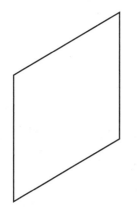

8.

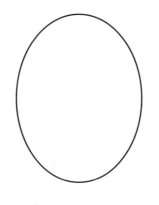

9.

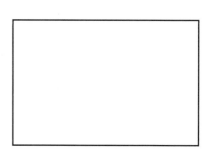

Answer Key

Page 1

1. 2 x 4 = 8   2. 2 x 5 = 10
3. 2 x 6 = 12   4. 3 x 6 = 18
5. 2 x 8 = 16   6. 2 x 7 = 14

Page 2

1. 2, 4, 6, 8, 10   12, 14, 16, 18   2. 3, 6, 9, 12   18, 21, 24, 27

3. 1, 2, 3, 4, 5   6, 7, 8, 9   4. 0, 0, 0, 0   0, 0, 0, 0

Page 3

1. 4, 8, 12, 16, 20   24, 28, 32, 36   2. 5, 10, 15, 20   30, 35, 40, 45

3. 6, 12, 18, 24, 30   36, 42, 48, 54   4. 7, 14, 21, 28   42, 49, 56, 63

5. 20   6. 0
7. 9   8. 20
9. 35   10. 21
11. 5   12. 32
13. 18   14. 45
15. 14   16. 10

Page 4

1. 8, 16, 24, 32, 40   48, 56, 64, 72   2. 9, 18, 27, 36, 45   54, 63, 72, 81

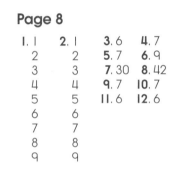

x	0	1	2	3	4	5	6	7	8	9
0	0	0	0	0	0	0	0	0	0	0
1	0	1	2	3	4	5	6	7	8	9
2	0	2	4	6	8	10	12	14	16	18
3	0	3	6	9	12	15	18	21	24	27
4	0	4	8	12	16	20	24	28	32	36
5	0	5	10	15	20	25	30	35	40	45
6	0	6	12	18	24	30	36	42	48	54
7	0	7	14	21	28	35	42	49	56	63
8	0	8	16	24	32	40	48	56	64	72
9	0	9	18	27	36	45	54	63	72	81

Page 5

1. 3, 12 ÷ 4 = 3
2. 5, 15 ÷ 3 = 5
3. 10, 10, 5, 10 ÷ 2 = 5
4. 12, 12, 3, 12 ÷ 4 = 3
5. 18, 6, 18 ÷ 3 = 6
6. 24, 4, 24 ÷ 6 = 4

Page 6

1. 4, 8 ÷ 2 = 4
2. 5, 10 ÷ 2 = 5
3. 7, 14 ÷ 2 = 7
4. 6, 12 ÷ 2 = 6
5. 6, 18 ÷ 3 = 6
6. 7, 21 ÷ 3 = 7

Page 7

1. 1   2. 1   3. 2   4. 2
   2   2   5. 5   6. 3
   3   3   7. 5   8. 7
   4   4   9. 4   10. 4
   5   5   11. 5   12. 9
   6   6   13. 2   14. 2
   7   7   15. 4   16. 6
   8   8   17. 7   18. 7
   9   9

Page 8

1. 1   2. 1   3. 6   4. 7
   2   2   5. 7   6. 9
   3   3   7. 30   8. 42
   4   4   9. 7   10. 7
   5   5   11. 6   12. 6
   6   6
   7   7
   8   8
   9   9

Page 9

1. 1   2. 1   3. 40   4. 4   5. 63
   2   2   6. 3   7. 7   8. 28
   3   3   9. 42   10. 36   11. 7
   4   4   12. 5   13. 56   14. 8
   5   5   15. 49   16. 9   17. 8
   6   6   18. 36   19. 1   20. 6
   7   7
   8   8
   9   9

Page 10

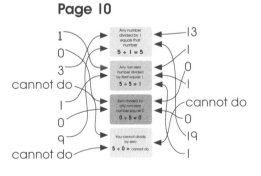

Page 11

1. 4)32 = 8   2. 2)18 = 9
3. 7)28 = 4   4. 6)48 = 8

5. 6   6. 5
7. 9   8. 6
9. 8   10. 1
11. 7   12. 8   13. 8
14. 7   15. 7   16. 3
17. 9   18. 7   19. 0

Page 12

1. 16   2. 0   3. 45   4. 32   5. 30
6. 7   7. 9   8. 7   9. 9   10. 8
11. 35   12. 49   13. 54   14. 5   15. 63
16. 0   17. 9   18. 6   19. 8   20. cannot do
21. 28 ÷ 7 = 4 stickers

Page 13

1. 36 ribbons
2. 35 hours
3. 24 bottles

Page 14

1. 3 birds
2. 5 loaves
3. 5 bananas
4. 7 lions

Page 15

1. (divide) 3 pounds
2. (multiply) 27 cards
3. (divide) 7 babies
4. (divide) 16 flowers

30

Answer Key

Page 16

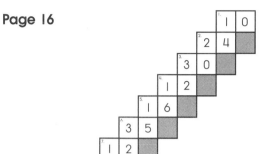

Page 17

1. a - 6
   b - 8
2. a - 32
   b - 37
3. a - 8
   b - 24

Page 18

1. a - 12
   b - 3
2. a - 28
   b - 7
3. a - 7
   b - 35

Page 19

1. a - 30
   b - 2
2. a - 22
   b - 11
3. a - 10
   b - 7

Page 20

1. $\frac{1}{3}$
2. $\frac{4}{5}$
3. $\frac{2}{6}$
4. $\frac{1}{7}$
5. $\frac{7}{8}$
6. $\frac{9}{12}$
7. $\frac{3}{4}$
8. $\frac{6}{8}$
9. $\frac{2}{10}$

Page 21

1. 2
2. 8
3. 5
4. 24
5. 2

Page 22

1. 4   2. 7   3. 1   4. 34
5. 2   6. 4   7. 5   8. 16
9. =   10. <   11. >

Page 23

1.  10:00
2. 8:34
3.  6:05
4.  7:59

Page 24

1. 8:10
2. 1:38
3. 6:58

Page 25

1. 8:15
2. 9:55
3. 3:35

Page 26

1. square
2. rhombus
3. rectangle
4. rhombus
5. rectangle
6. square
7.
8.
9.

Page 27

1.
2.
3.
4.
5.
6.
7.
8.
9.

Page 28

1.
2.
3.
4.
5.
6.
7.
8.
9.

Page 29

1.
2.
3.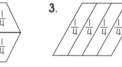
4.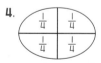
5.
6.
7.
8.
9.

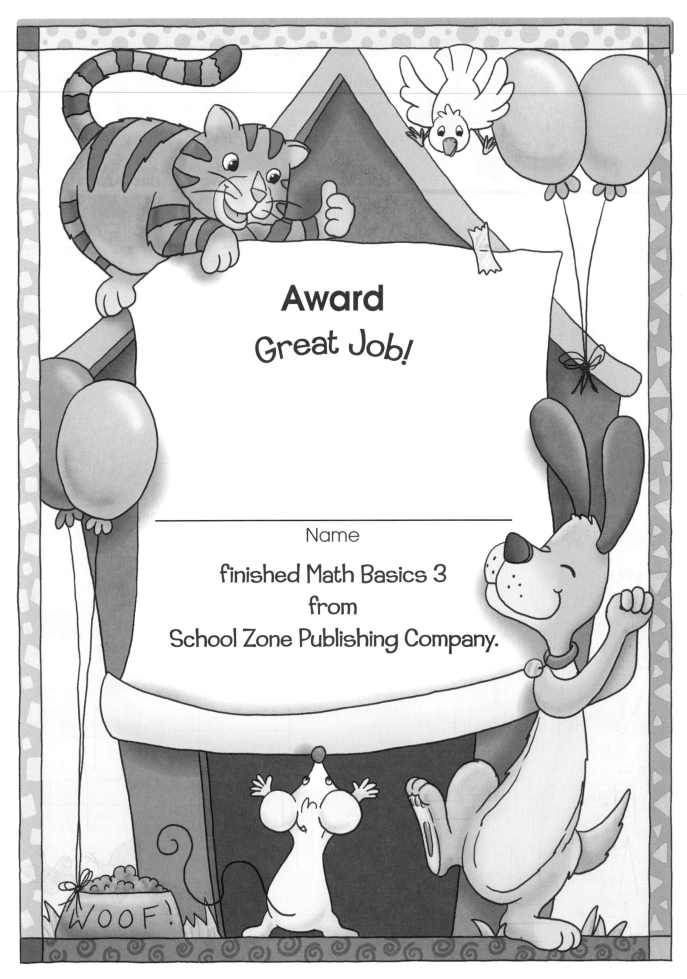

Award
Great Job!

_____
Name

finished Math Basics 3
from
School Zone Publishing Company.